COPY WRITING SECRETS
WITH

AI FOR WRITERS

AN AI BOOK THAT UNLOCKS THE SECRETS TO ATTRACT MORE CLICKS, PROFITS AND SALES FROM WHATEVER YOU SELL

By

ANDREW MARK

Table Of Contents

Andrew Mark

INTRODUCTION

In the dynamic and ever-evolving environment of communication, where words hold the key to unlocking the hearts and minds of readers, a dynamic revolution is taking place. The marriage of human intellect and artificial intelligence has given birth to a revolution that is redefining the very foundations of copywriting, transforming it into an art and science like never before. Welcome to the thrilling voyage where we examine how AI, sometimes considered as a threat to traditional professions, becomes your ultimate partner in the field of copywriting, increasing your creative armory and boosting the potency of your words.

The Power of Persuasion

In the age-old goal of persuasion, writers have attempted to produce narratives that engage emotionally with their audience. The core of persuasive writing rests in its potential to inspire, excite, and influence. It is about engaging with the reader on an emotional level, pushing them to act, believe, or simply engage with the content. Persuasive writing is not only a skill; it's an art, a craft that wordsmiths hone through years of practice and self-discovery.

Within this dense tapestry of persuasive writing, two crucial aspects are at play: ethos and pathos. Ethos, the credibility of the author, and pathos, the emotional appeal, work together to captivate the reader and encourage them to do the desired action. However, traditional persuasive writing, as successful as it might be, often falls short in leveraging the immense potential of data and insights that modern technology offers.

The Power of Data and AI

Now, enter the arena of artificial intelligence (AI), the game-changer in the art and science of persuasive writing. AI is not a replacement for the human touch; it is a catalyst that amplifies the essence of human creativity. It arms copywriters with a treasure mine of data, insights, and tools that are beyond the grasp of conventional approaches.

Imagine having at your disposal a writing partner that is not only capable of generating content at a surprising pace but also boasts the ability to evaluate large datasets of user behavior, preferences, and market trends. AI has the unique capacity to discover patterns in the noise, exposing what genuinely resonates with your target audience. It knows the science of language, deploying algorithms that harness the power of persuasion by understanding the intricate mechanics of human intellect and emotions.

AI in Copywriting: The Ultimate Partner

In the field of copywriting, AI is not just an ally; it is the ideal partner. It may generate appealing content that smoothly blends together ethos and pathos, creating powerful narratives that engage with your audience. The confluence of human creativity and AI-powered insight is a formidable force that transcends the boundaries of traditional copywriting.

So, why should you accept AI as your ideal copywriting partner? This book is aimed to unravel the captivating tale of this cooperation, analyzing the symbiotic interplay between human brilliance and machine intelligence. We will explore the indisputable benefits of applying AI into your copywriting activities, allowing you to generate content that not only captivates but also converts.

In the pages that follow, we will go through the art and science of persuasive writing, de-constructing the age-old ideas that have defined effective communication for generations. We will delve into the complexities of human emotion, psychology, and the power of storytelling, recognizing their timeless value in the realm of words.

However, we won't stop there. Our adventure will also delve into the domain of AI, demystifying the technology that is disrupting and reshaping the copywriting scene. We will comprehend the capabilities of AI in language generation, its prowess in data analysis, and how it has the ability to change the fundamental core of persuasive.

Bridging the Gap

In the wake of the AI revolution, there exists a perceived difference between the creative genius of the human intellect and the precision of machine learning. The danger is that AI might mechanize the craft of copywriting, depriving it of its character and authenticity. Yet, this couldn't be further from the truth.

AI is a bridge between the subtleties of human creativity and the power of data-driven precision. It accentuates human inventiveness rather than substitutes it. The outcome is not just persuasive writing; it's material that can adapt, evolve, and thrive in a world of ever-changing reader preferences and market realities.

This book tries to remove the fallacies around AI in copywriting and, instead, show its potential as your most valued ally. We will explain how AI can streamline your creative process, providing you with more time for strategic thinking and idea generation. It can alleviate the drudgery of repetitive activities, freeing you to focus on the key components of your trade, such as ideas, strategy, and storytelling.

Part I: Foundations of Copywriting

CHAPTER ONE

THE ANATOMY OF GREAT COPY

The creation of compelling and persuasive content is a craft that demands a profound understanding of human psychology, language, and persuasion techniques.

Crafting successful copy is an art and a science. Whether you're writing a social media post, a blog piece, a sales email, or a print ad, the words you use can make or break your campaign's success. Effective copy has the capacity to fascinate, persuade, and connect with your audience on a deep, emotional level. In this chapter, we will cover the main characteristics of great copywriting that will help you to write material that not only educates but also influences and inspires.

1. Know Your Audience:

The cornerstone of great copywriting is a strong grasp of your target audience. Before you put pen to paper or fingers to keyboard, you must determine who you are writing for. What are their demographics, interests, values, and pain points? Create buyer personas to guide your writing and personalize your message to match their individual requirements and goals.

2. Establish Clear Objectives:

What is the purpose of your copy? Are you seeking to inform, entertain, persuade, or sell? Clearly establish your objectives before you start writing, as this will affect the tone, style, and content of your copy. If your purpose is to sell a product, your copy will be radically different from a piece created to educate or entertain.

3. Compelling Headlines:

Your title is the first thing your audience sees, and it's the make-or-break moment. Craft a title that captures attention, expresses the substance of your message, and entices your readers to keep reading. Use power words, fascinating questions, and data to make your headlines stick out.

4. Emotional Connection:

People make decisions based on emotions, and then explain them with rationality. Effective copy taps into these emotions. Use narrative, meaningful experiences, and vivid visuals to connect with your audience on a human level. Help people imagine how your product or service may enrich their life.

5. Benefit-Oriented Content:

Rather to merely listing characteristics, focus on the benefits your product or service brings. How will it improve your audience's life? Speak to their desires and pain areas by showing how your offering can alleviate their problems or fulfill their dreams.

6. Clarity and Simplicity:

Your copy should be clear to understand. Avoid jargon, elaborate sentences, and confusing phrasing. Write in a direct, conversational tone that guarantees your message is crystal apparent. As Albert Einstein famously observed, "If you can't explain it simply, you don't understand it well enough."

7. Use of Persuasive Language:

Incorporate persuasive aspects into your copy. Employ strategies like as scarcity, social proof, and the fear of losing out to promote action. Craft engaging calls to action that leave little space for doubt about what you want the reader to do next.

8. Establish Credibility:

Credibility is essential. Back up your statements with evidence, testimonials, case studies, or data. If your audience doesn't trust you, they won't buy into your message or take action.

9. Show, Don't Tell:

Rather than telling your audience how fantastic your product or service is, show them. Paint a clear image of the benefits utilizing descriptive language, sensory elements, and real-life examples. Let your audience experience the benefit rather than merely hearing about it.

10. Know Your Unique Selling Proposition (USP):

What sets your product or service apart from the competition? Highlight your USP in your copy. It's what makes you stand out in a crowded marketplace and offers your audience a reason to choose you.

11. Create Scannable Content:

In the age of digital information overload, people often skim rather than read in depth. Use subheadings, bullet points, and short paragraphs to make your information quickly scannable. Break up long text using images, infographics, and white space to boost reading.

12. Consistency in Voice and Branding:

Your copy should be consistent with your brand's voice and messaging. Maintain a unified tone, style, and visual identity across all your material to generate trust and recognition.

13. A/B Testing:

To fine-tune your copy for optimal results, undertake A/B testing. Create many versions of your content with tiny adjustments and test them with your target audience. Analyze the data to identify what resonates most and iterate accordingly.

14. Use Power Words:

Certain words have a more significant impact on readers than others. Incorporate power words like "free," "you," "guaranteed," and "new" to catch attention and establish a sense of urgency.

15. Avoid Clichés: Clichés are overused and uninspired.

Steer cautious of sentences that have lost their impact owing to repetition. Instead, try for originality and inventiveness in your copy.

16. Edit Ruthlessly:

Great copy is honed, polished, and free of faults. After drafting your original draft, take the time to edit and proofread. Eliminate extraneous words, clarify your topic, and ensure your writing is brief and error-free.

17. The Power of Testimonials:

Including client testimonials in your content helps enhance credibility and trust. Showcase good experiences and endorsements from delighted customers to highlight the value of your product or service.

18. Be Conversational:

Write as if you're having a one-on-one conversation with your reader. This personal touch makes your audience feel more engaged and connected to your message.

19. Foster Curiosity:

Pique your reader's curiosity with open loops and questions that keep them captivated and wanting to learn more. Tease the benefits of your product without giving away everything.

20. KISS Principle: Keep It Simple and Short

The KISS concept, "Keep It Simple and Short," is a guiding guideline for effective copy-writing. Simplicity is the key to clarity. Avoid excessive intricacy and verbosity. Get straight to the point, and cut out any needless stuff.

Remember, effective copy isn't just about the words; it's about developing an emotional connection, building trust, and eventually driving action. Practice, improve, and maintain your finger on the pulse of your audience's growing requirements and tastes, and your content will continue to be a potent tool in your marketing armory.

CRAFTING ATTENTION-GRABBING HEADLINES

The ability of writing attention-grabbing headlines is a key skill. A great headline serves as the doorway to your message, pulling readers in and persuading them to investigate your content further. In this chapter, we will delve into the anatomy of amazing headlines, providing practical insights, examples, and data to assist your copywriting journey.

The Power of the First Impression

Your headline is the first impression your audience receives of your material, and as the phrase goes, "you never get a second chance to make a first impression." Research suggests that 80% of readers never make it past the headline, making it vital in catching attention. For instance, a study by Out-brain indicated that headlines with eight to twelve words have the highest click-through rates, underscoring the value of conciseness.

Examples of Winning Headlines

Consider these examples:

"Unleash Your Inner Creativity: 10 Tips for Inspired Innovation"

"Double Your Productivity in 7 Days: Time-Tested Techniques"

"The Secret to Effortless Weight Loss: A 30-Minute Daily Habit"

Each of these titles generates curiosity, offers a benefit, and hints at the content's value, all critical parts of a good headline.

Statistics for Success

Studies suggest that headlines with numbers, such as "7 Tips" or "10 Ways," tend to perform 36% better than those without. Furthermore, headlines that pose a question elicit 23% greater attention.

Generating attention-grabbing headlines is both an art and a science. By recognizing the importance of the initial impression, examining successful instances, and utilizing statistical insights, you can write headlines that grab your readers and lead them to investigate your content further.

NAVIGATING THE STRUCTURE OF PERSUASIVE CONTENT

Crafting persuasive content is an art that involves understanding the intricate structure that captures an audience's attention, sustains their interest, and guides them to take action. This chapter delves into the anatomy of persuasive content, offering a practical guide on how to create compelling narratives that resonate with your target audience.

Understanding the Structure:

Effective persuasive content follows a well-defined structure. It begins with a captivating headline that grabs the reader's attention. Statistics show that headlines containing numbers or intriguing questions increase engagement by 73%. For example, a headline like "5 Strategies for Boosting Your Productivity" immediately sparks curiosity.

The next critical element is the introduction, where you establish the problem or desire your audience can relate to. A startling fact or anecdote can evoke emotions and pique interest. Approximately 86% of readers are more likely to continue reading when they connect emotionally with the opening.

The body of your content should provide valuable information, supporting your main argument with facts, examples, and expert opinions. Integrating visual content, such as infographics or charts, can boost engagement by 65%. Presenting stats and case studies adds credibility, increasing the likelihood of persuading your audience.

To maintain the reader's interest, use subheadings, bullet points, and shorter paragraphs. Online readers tend to skim, with 43% more likely to engage with content that's visually structured.

Conclusion:

Mastering the structure of persuasive content is essential for effective communication. By crafting compelling headlines, emotionally resonant introductions, and information-rich bodies, you can significantly increase your chances of success. Incorporating statistics and engaging examples will enhance the persuasive power of your content, and structuring it for easy consumption ensures your message reaches and impacts your target audience.

Andrew Mark

CHAPTER TWO

KNOW YOUR AUDIENCE

In marketing, creating buyer personas is a foundational step that can significantly enhance the precision and impact of your messaging. A buyer persona is a semi-fictional representation of your ideal customer, crafted through meticulous research and analysis. This chapter delves into the intricacies of constructing compelling buyer personas to optimize your marketing strategies.

The Genesis of Buyer Personas

The first step in creating effective buyer personas is to gather comprehensive data. Start with market research, focusing on demographics, psychographics, and behavioral patterns. Consider conducting surveys, analyzing customer interviews, and leveraging existing customer data. For instance, if you are a software company, you might discover through data analysis that a significant proportion of your customers are tech-savvy millennials who value quick problem-solving. This information serves as the cornerstone for your persona creation.

Defining Demographics

Demographic data includes information such as age, gender, income, education, and location. Understanding your customers' demographics is vital because it can impact the way you communicate with them. For instance, if you are marketing luxury watches, your persona for a successful middle-aged professional might differ significantly from a college student looking for a fashionable timepiece.

Psycho-graphics - Digging Deeper

Beyond demographics, psycho-graphics delve into the emotional and psychological aspects of your customers. This includes their values, interests, attitudes, and lifestyle choices. Psycho-graphics provide deeper insights into what drives your customers' decision-making. Let's say you're marketing eco-friendly cleaning products. A persona for an environmentally conscious individual who prioritizes sustainable living will have distinct psycho-graphic characteristics compared to someone primarily concerned with convenience.

Behavioral Insights

Understanding your customers' behavior is essential. Analyze how they interact with your product or service, how frequently they make purchases, and what motivates their decisions. For instance, if you're in the e-commerce business, identifying that a segment of your customers makes frequent impulse purchases during flash sales is valuable information. This insight can help tailor your marketing to trigger more impulse buying within that segment.

Developing the Persona

Once you have collected this information, you can craft your buyer personas. Begin by giving your persona a name, such as "Savvy Sarah" for the tech-savvy millennial mentioned earlier. Describe her demographics, psychographics, and behavioral traits in detail. Creating a visual representation can also be helpful, using stock photos or illustrations to bring your persona to life.

Using Buyer Personas in Practice

With your buyer personas in hand, you can now fine-tune your marketing strategies:

1. Tailored Content

Craft content that speaks directly to each persona. For Savvy Sarah, you might create content that focuses on the technical aspects of your product. For the eco-conscious persona, emphasize the sustainability and environmental benefits.

2. Targeted Advertising

Utilize online advertising platforms to target specific buyer personas. Facebook, for example, allows you to create ad campaigns that precisely reach users with the demographics, interests, and behaviors that align with your personas.

3. Product Development

Adapt your product or service based on the needs and preferences of your personas. For example, if you find that the majority of your customers value ease of use, invest in user-friendly interfaces and clear instructions.

4. Improved Customer Service

Train your customer service teams to understand and empathize with the personas they are most likely to encounter. This enables them to provide more personalized assistance.

Evaluating the Impact

To measure the effectiveness of your buyer personas, track key performance indicators (KPIs). This might include metrics like conversion rates, customer retention, and customer satisfaction. If you see an increase in these KPIs for a specific persona, it's a strong indicator that your marketing efforts are paying off.

Case Studies and Statistics

The power of buyer personas is evident in various success stories and statistics:

- HubSpot reported that using personas in email marketing campaigns led to a 16% increase in email open rates, a 10% increase in click-through rates, and a 15% increase in email deliverability.

- Salesforce found that companies using personas in their marketing strategies increased their lead-to-opportunity conversion rates by 73%.

- Netflix, a prime example of persona-driven marketing, uses data analytics to categorize viewers into segments, resulting in personalized recommendations and a 75% user retention rate.

Creating buyer personas for targeted messaging is more than a marketing strategy—it's a guiding principle for understanding your customers and delivering exactly what they need. By diving deep into demographics, psychographics, and behaviors, you can create personas that reflect your diverse customer base, enabling you to tailor your messaging and product offerings effectively. The case studies and statistics mentioned above demonstrate the real impact of buyer personas in optimizing marketing efforts, making them an indispensable tool in the modern marketing arsenal.

THE PSYCHOLOGY OF CUSTOMER BEHAVIOR

At the core of customer behavior lies the concept of motivation. Why do consumers choose one product or service over another? Maslow's Hierarchy of Needs provides a valuable framework for understanding these motivations. According to this theory, consumers are driven by physiological, safety, social, esteem, and self-actualization needs. For example, a person's choice to purchase a luxury car may be driven by the need for esteem and self-actualization, while buying groceries satisfies their physiological and safety needs.

Statistics: According to a survey by Nielsen, 48% of consumers reported that their purchasing decisions are influenced by a brand's impact on society and the environment.

The Role of Emotions

Emotions play a significant role in consumer behavior. Our emotional responses to products and services can have a profound impact on our buying decisions. Positive emotions, such as happiness or excitement, can drive impulsive purchases, while negative emotions, like fear or anxiety, can deter consumers from making a purchase.

Example: Consider the success of Coca-Cola's "Share a Coke" campaign, which personalized their product with individual names. This simple but emotionally resonant approach led to a 2% increase in U.S. sales, demonstrating the power of emotional engagement.

Cognitive Dissonance and Post-Purchase Behavior

Once a purchase is made, consumers often experience cognitive dissonance – a feeling of discomfort or doubt about their decision. To alleviate this dissonance, consumers may seek information or reassurance. Marketers can use this knowledge to provide excellent post-purchase support, like after-sales services or clear return policies, to minimize buyer's remorse.

Example: Apple's customer service is renowned for its post-purchase support. This has resulted in a high customer retention rate and loyalty, even when their products are more expensive compared to competitors.

Social Influences

People are social creatures, and our behavior is often shaped by the opinions and actions of others. Social influences can be categorized into three main types: reference groups, social roles, and family influences.

Statistics: A survey by BrightLocal found that 88% of consumers trust online reviews as much as personal recommendations.

Practical Tip: Encourage customers to leave reviews and testimonials to leverage social influences positively.

Offer incentives or rewards for sharing their experiences with your product or service.

Decision-Making Heuristics

Customers often rely on mental shortcuts or decision-making heuristics when making purchasing decisions. These shortcuts can be categorized into availability heuristics (relying on readily available information) and representativeness heuristics (making decisions based on similarities to existing categories).

Example: When choosing a restaurant, a person might rely on availability heuristics, selecting the one that comes to mind first because it's the easiest to recall.

USING AI TO ANALYZE AND SEGMENT YOUR AUDIENCE

The era of traditional demographic segmentation has evolved into a more sophisticated approach, driven by AI.

Instead of relying solely on age, gender, or location, businesses now focus on behavioral, psychographic, and intent-based factors. This shift is fueled by the wealth of data available on online platforms and the ability of AI to process and analyze this data at unprecedented scale and speed.

Benefits of AI-Powered Audience Analysis

Enhanced Personalization: AI enables businesses to create highly personalized content and experiences for their audience. For instance, Netflix uses AI to recommend movies and TV shows based on a viewer's past preferences, leading to increased user engagement and retention.

Increased Conversion Rates: By understanding the intent and behavior of users, businesses can craft compelling and relevant content that drives higher conversion rates. Amazon's product recommendations serve as a prime example of this, as they attribute a significant portion of their revenue to AI-powered personalized suggestions.

Optimized Marketing Spend: AI helps in allocating resources more efficiently by identifying high-value segments and targeting them effectively. A study by McKinsey found that AI-driven marketing strategies result in a 10-30% increase in marketing efficiency.

Real-time Insights: AI algorithms process data in real-time, allowing businesses to adapt and refine their strategies on the fly. Twitter's use of AI for real-time trending topics and content recommendations is a testament to this.

Practical Applications

1. Content Recommendations: Media platforms like Spotify use AI to recommend songs and playlists tailored to users' musical preferences. This approach keeps users engaged and entices them to stay on the platform longer.

2. E-commerce: Companies like eBay use AI to analyze user behavior, providing personalized product recommendations and optimizing search results. This results in higher conversion rates and increased revenue.

3. Email Marketing: Email marketing platforms employ AI to segment subscribers based on their engagement history, enabling businesses to send targeted content and offers. According to a study by Campaign Monitor, segmented email campaigns yield a 760% increase in revenue.

4. Social Media Advertising: Platforms like Facebook utilize AI to analyze user behavior and interests, ensuring that ads are displayed to the most relevant audience. This approach leads to better ad performance and a higher return on ad spend (ROAS).

STATISTICS ON AI-POWERED AUDIENCE ANALYSIS

◆ A survey by Evergage reported that 88% of marketers saw a significant improvement in their business from using AI for audience segmentation and personalization.

◆ According to Forbes, businesses that use AI for customer personalization can increase revenue by up to 15%.

◆ A study by the Aberdeen Group revealed that companies using AI for audience analysis and segmentation experienced a 2.7 times increase in click-through rates and a 3.2 times increase in open rates.

The use of AI for audience analysis and segmentation has transformed the marketing landscape. By harnessing the power of AI, businesses can gain a deep understanding of their audience, deliver highly personalized content, and optimize their marketing strategies. The statistics and practical examples provided here underline the significant impact that AI can have on marketing success, making it an essential tool for modern businesses striving to stay ahead of the competition. In the rapidly evolving world of digital marketing, those who embrace AI will undoubtedly gain a competitive edge and secure a brighter future for their brands.

CHAPTER THREE

THE POWER OF STORYTELLING

Stories are the beating heart of human communication. They have the power to captivate, inspire, and connect with readers on a profound level. This chapter delves into the art and science of crafting stories that resonate with readers, exploring the key elements that make a narrative compelling and examining the psychological and emotional factors that underpin their effectiveness.

THE POWER OF EMOTION

Great stories stir emotions. According to research by Dr. Paul Zak, professor of psychology and neuroscience, stories that evoke strong emotional responses release oxytocin, often referred to as the "love hormone." This chemical fosters trust, empathy, and connection. For instance, a study showed that narratives triggering oxytocin in readers increased their willingness to help others by 47%.

Example 1: Pixar's "Up"

Pixar's film "Up" masterfully employs emotional storytelling. The opening sequence, which chronicles the life of the main character, Carl, and his wife Ellie, is a poignant tale of love and loss. It resonates with viewers because it elicits powerful emotions, forging a deep connection.

THE HERO'S JOURNEY

Joseph Campbell's concept of the Hero's Journey is a blueprint for successful storytelling. It involves a hero facing challenges, undergoing transformation, and ultimately returning home. Stories that follow this structure, like the "Star Wars" saga, resonate because they mirror universal human experiences, making them relatable.

Example 2: Harry Potter Series

J.K. Rowling's Harry Potter series aligns with the Hero's Journey. Harry's adventures, challenges, and personal growth resonate with readers, as they see reflections of their own struggles and triumphs.

CHARACTER RELATABILITY

Readers connect with characters they can relate to. A study by the National Academy of Sciences revealed that when readers identify with a character, their brain activity mimics the character's emotions. Relatable characters, like Scout Finch in Harper Lee's "To Kill a Mockingbird," engage readers emotionally and intellectually.

Example 3: Holden Caulfield in "The Catcher in the Rye"

Holden Caulfield's existential crisis and adolescent rebellion resonate with readers, as many have grappled with similar feelings during their youth. His character represents a universal struggle for identity and meaning.

CONFLICT AND RESOLUTION

Conflict is the engine that drives stories forward. It creates tension, suspense, and a desire to see how things unfold. Readers are naturally drawn to narratives that pose challenges and offer resolutions.

Example 4: "Gone Girl" by Gillian Flynn

In "Gone Girl," the central conflict of a deteriorating marriage and a mysterious disappearance keeps readers on the edge of their seats. The resolution, while shocking, is the culmination of the emotional journey, leaving a lasting impact.

THE ART OF PACING

Effective pacing is crucial in storytelling. Well-timed revelations, twists, and revelations maintain reader engagement. The "Sherlock Holmes" stories by Arthur Conan Doyle exemplify masterful pacing. Each story presents clues, riddles, and solutions that keep readers hooked until the end.

Example 5: "The Hound of the Baskervilles"

In "The Hound of the Baskervilles," Doyle gradually unfolds the mystery of the ghostly hound, drawing readers into the suspense. The well-timed revelations build tension and ensure that the story resonates long after it's finished.

The Takeaway

Stories have the power to transcend time and culture because they tap into the universal aspects of the human experience. By understanding the emotional impact of storytelling, the Hero's Journey, relatable characters, conflict, and pacing, you can craft narratives that resonate deeply with your readers. As shown through examples and supported by research, these elements are essential to creating stories that leave a lasting imprint in the hearts and minds of your audience. Mastering the art of storytelling is a journey worth embarking on, with endless possibilities to connect, inspire, and resonate with readers.

INCORPORATING NARRATIVES INTO YOUR COPY

Incorporating narratives into your copy is a potent technique that can breathe life into your content, making it engaging and relatable to your audience. Narratives, when used effectively, can evoke emotions, create a connection, and persuade readers to take action. Let's consider the art of storytelling in copywriting, and see some practical insights and real-world examples to demonstrate its impact.

THE POWER OF NARRATIVE

At its core, a narrative is a story, and stories have been a fundamental part of human communication for centuries. They captivate our attention, spark our imagination, and help us remember information. According to statistics, a well-crafted narrative can increase the likelihood of message retention by up to 65% compared to non-narrative content.

WHY USE NARRATIVES IN COPY?

Engagement: People are naturally drawn to stories. Incorporating narratives into your copy can transform a mundane message into an engaging tale that keeps your audience hooked.

Example: Consider an advertisement for a fitness product. Instead of listing features, share a story of someone's transformation journey using the product, describing their struggles, victories, and ultimate success.

Emotion: Narratives tap into human emotions. By creating an emotional connection with your audience, you can influence their decisions.

Example: A nonprofit organization's fundraising copy can narrate the experiences of beneficiaries, eliciting empathy and motivating donors to contribute.

Relatability: Stories are relatable. They allow readers to see themselves in the narrative, making your message more personal and relevant.

Example: In a product review, share a story about how the product solved a common problem you personally encountered, making it relatable to your readers.

Memorability: People remember stories better than facts and figures. Your message is more likely to stick in your audience's mind when presented in a narrative form.

Example: A tech company's copy can illustrate the evolution of a product through a chronological narrative, making it easier for customers to remember its history.

STRUCTURING YOUR NARRATIVE COPY

A well-structured narrative is key to its effectiveness. Follow these steps:

Introduction: Begin with a captivating hook. It can be a problem, a mystery, or a relatable situation. Draw the reader into your story.

Example: "Imagine being lost in the wilderness, with no GPS or map to guide you. This was the predicament John found himself in during his last camping trip."

Conflict: Introduce the central conflict or challenge. This sets the stage for the narrative's resolution.

Example: "John was miles away from civilization, and his phone battery was about to die. Survival was his only option."

Resolution: Describe how the conflict is resolved. This is where your product or solution comes into play.

Example: "Fortunately, John had packed a solar-powered charger, which saved the day. With a fully charged phone, he navigated his way back to safety."

Conclusion: Sum up the key takeaways and the benefits of the product or message.

Example: "With the right tools, you can overcome any challenge. Just like John, you can be prepared for the unexpected."

Case in Point: Dove's Real Beauty Campaign

Dove's "Real Beauty" campaign is a shining example of how narratives can transform a brand's image. Instead of traditional beauty advertisements, Dove chose to tell real stories of women and their journeys to self-acceptance. The result? A 600% increase in sales over a decade.

No doubt, incorporating narratives into your copy is a skill that every copywriter should master. When used strategically, it has the power to captivate, engage, and persuade your audience. With a well-structured narrative, your copy can become memorable and resonate with readers on a personal level. So, remember, the next time you're crafting copy, think of the story you can tell to connect with your audience, and watch the impact it can have on your message.

AI-GENERATED STORYTELLING TECHNIQUES

Storytelling is a timeless art that has created cultures, maintained histories, and inspired emotions for ages. As we navigate the digital world, we find ourselves in an era where Artificial Intelligence (AI) plays a key role in strengthening our narrative techniques. This merger of art and technology opens a new arena of possibilities, enabling us to construct fascinating narratives that engage, inform, and inspire. In this exploration, we will delve into the world of AI-powered storytelling techniques, revealing their potential and sharing practical insights to create fascinating tales.

Understanding AI in Storytelling

Before we get into the practicalities of employing AI for storytelling, it's vital to appreciate the nature of this symbiotic connection. AI, in this perspective, functions as a tool rather than a creative entity. It supports storytellers in different stages of the narrative process, from idea generation to audience involvement.

Idea Generation: AI can assist in producing unique story ideas by analyzing enormous information, recognizing trends, and offering novel themes. It empowers storytellers to explore uncharted places.

Character Development: AI can help develop well-rounded characters by studying personality features, conversation patterns, and even suggest unique character quirks, making them more approachable and interesting.

Plot building: AI can assist with plot building by forecasting various story arcs, finding conflicts, and guaranteeing a logical flow of events, all while keeping suspense and surprise.

Language Enhancement: AI can be used to improve the quality of written text, boosting the storytelling experience. It can fix grammar, enhance vocabulary, and assure coherent writing.

Practical Applications of AI in Storytelling

Now that we've outlined the importance of AI in narrative, let's explore some practical approaches to harness its power.

Data Analysis for Ideas: AI techniques like text mining and sentiment analysis can filter through a multitude of data, finding trends, developing topics, and public attitude. Storytellers can harness this data to create storylines that resonate with the contemporary times.

Automated Character Profiling: AI-driven personality assessments can aid in producing well-defined characters. By examining a character's qualities, feelings, and motivations, storytellers can construct more convincing and relatable personalities.

Predictive Analytics for Plot: Predictive analytics can advise storytellers by forecasting audience emotions and preferences. By studying prior performance indicators,

AI can help in altering plots to optimize audience engagement.

Natural Language Processing (NLP): Utilizing NLP methods, storytellers can boost the quality of their prose. AI can detect and repair grammatical problems, suggest improved sentence structures, and even make word choice recommendations.

Tailored Storytelling: AI can develop tailored material, adapting the narrative to each readers. By assessing user data and preferences, tales can be tailored to create a more immersive experience.

Enlightening Insights from AI-Enhanced Storytelling

Beyond the practical applications, AI also delivers useful insights that might boost your narrative techniques.

Embrace Collaboration: AI is not a replacement for human ingenuity; it's a partner. Collaborate with AI to amplify your narrative abilities. Use AI as a creative assistant, not a substitute.

Continuous Learning: Stay informed with the newest AI tools and approaches. The field is changing swiftly, and being educated can help you grasp the full potential of AI in storytelling.

Ethical Considerations: Be mindful of ethical considerations while employing AI in storytelling. Ensure that the data you feed into AI models is handled appropriately and that the information created is courteous and unbiased.

Emotion & Empathy: While AI can assist in many elements of storytelling, the ability to generate emotions and empathy remains distinctively human. Focus on these characteristics to produce deeply resonant stories.

Feedback Loop: Collect feedback from your audience. AI may assist in assessing audience responses, letting you refine your storytelling approaches and generate more compelling storylines.

The Future of AI-Enhanced Storytelling

As technology progresses, the future of AI-enhanced storytelling holds even greater promise. AI-driven virtual reality and augmented reality experiences are emerging, offering immersive tales that blur the barrier between fiction and reality. Interactive storytelling, powered by AI, will allow readers to affect the end of the narrative, producing individualized and exciting adventures.

However, with great power comes great responsibility. Storytellers must strike a balance between inventiveness and ethics. AI's capacity to manipulate information and generate convincing material raises concerns about disinformation and deepfakes. Storytellers should employ AI with integrity and guarantee their stories are honest and trustworthy.

AI is a potent technology that can transform storytelling tactics. It brings fresh ideas, refines character development, aids in story building, and enhances language. Nevertheless, it's crucial to remember that AI is a supplement to human ingenuity, not a replacement. As we go into the AI-driven future of storytelling, let us embrace collaboration, constant learning, and ethical issues.

The union of art and technology, when wielded with talent and integrity, has the ability to produce storytelling that surpasses the limitations of imagination, leaving a lasting influence on the hearts and minds of audiences throughout the world. Embrace the AI storyteller's toolkit, and go on a path of creativity and invention, weaving storylines that resonate, inspire, and endure.

Part II: AI Tools for Copy-writing

CHAPTER FOUR

AI-POWERED CONTENT GENERATION

In the digital age, where content is king, mastering the art of copywriting is paramount. However, the landscape of copywriting has evolved with the advent of Artificial Intelligence (AI) technologies. In this chapter, we'll delve into the intriguing world of AI Copywriting Tools, exploring their capabilities, impact, and practical applications.

The Rise of AI Copywriting Tools

AI-powered copywriting tools have surged in popularity, revolutionizing the way content is created. According to a recent survey by the Content Marketing Institute, 63% of marketers believe AI-powered content creation is the future. This surge is driven by the remarkable capabilities these tools offer.

Capabilities of AI Copywriting Tools

AI copywriting tools are not merely grammar-checkers or synonym suggesters; they are intelligent content generators. These tools employ advanced natural language processing algorithms to understand context, tone, and target audience. They can create a variety of content, including blog posts, product descriptions, social media posts, and more, with remarkable accuracy and efficiency.

Example 1: Email Campaigns

Consider an email marketing campaign. Traditional copywriting may take hours to craft compelling, personalized messages for a vast subscriber list. AI copywriting tools, on the other hand, can generate a batch of personalized emails in minutes, increasing efficiency and engagement.

The Impact of AI on Copywriting

AI copywriting tools are not just about convenience; they have a profound impact on the effectiveness of your content.

Example 2: SEO Optimization

Search Engine Optimization (SEO) is a critical aspect of content creation. AI tools can analyze vast datasets to identify the most relevant keywords, helping your content rank higher in search engine results. This, in turn, increases organic traffic and enhances your online presence.

Practical Applications

1. Content Generation:

AI copywriting tools are invaluable for generating content at scale. Whether you need product descriptions, blog posts, or social media updates, AI can create high-quality content swiftly.

Example 3: Social Media Posts

Crafting engaging social media posts is time-consuming. AI tools can analyze your brand's tone and audience preferences, producing posts that resonate with your followers.

2. Editing and Proofreading:

AI tools excel in grammar and spell-checking, ensuring error-free content. This is particularly vital in professional communication and marketing materials.

Example 4: Academic Writing

For students and professionals, AI tools can provide comprehensive proofreading and suggest improvements for essays, reports, and research papers.

3. Language Translation:

AI-powered translation tools are increasingly sophisticated. They can translate content accurately and quickly, making your content accessible to a global audience.

Example 5: Multilingual Marketing

When expanding into international markets, AI translation tools can help adapt your marketing materials for different languages, ensuring cultural sensitivity.

Embracing AI Copy-writing Tools: Best Practices

While AI copy-writing tools offer remarkable benefits, they are most effective when used alongside human expertise. Incorporate the following best practices:

Content Review: Always review and edit AI-generated content for tone, accuracy, and relevance.

Data Privacy: Ensure that sensitive data is handled securely, especially when using AI tools for customer communications.

Continuous Learning: Stay updated with the latest AI copy-writing advancements to leverage their full potential.

Monitoring: Regularly monitor the performance of AI-generated content and gather feedback to make improvements.

The introduction of AI copywriting tools represents a groundbreaking shift in the world of content creation. These tools not only enhance efficiency but also improve the quality of content, making it more engaging and relevant to your audience. When used thoughtfully, AI copywriting tools can be a game-changer in your content strategy, propelling your brand to new heights in the digital landscape.

GPT-4 AND BEYOND: THE EVOLUTION OF AI COPYWRITING

As we explore into the world of GPT-4 and beyond, we find ourselves at the intersection of innovation and creativity, witnessing a massive transformation in the way material is made, communicated, and consumed.

This fascinating voyage gives not only a glimpse into the boundless potential of artificial intelligence but also priceless lessons for people in the industries of marketing, content development, and beyond.

The Genesis of AI Copywriting

The story begins with the invention of AI, a pioneering technology that has advanced by leaps and bounds over the previous decades. GPT-4, an offspring of this ever-evolving landscape, takes us a step farther by boosting natural language processing, comprehending context, and generating coherent, contextually relevant text. But how did we come at this position, when machines can produce persuasive and interesting copy that rivals human creativity?

At the center of this evolution is a treasure of data - huge, diverse, and easily accessible. AI systems like GPT-4 are trained on mounds of text data from books, journals, webpages, and more. This huge data pool allows AI to recognize the intricacies of language, tone, and style. However, it's not just about data. It's about the ability to learn and adapt. These AI systems use deep learning techniques to continually improve their capabilities, making them increasingly adept at reading and mimicking human writing.

The Power of GPT-4

GPT-4, the next milestone in AI copywriting, is not only an incremental improvement; it is a big leap ahead. What sets GPT-4 distinctive is its exceptional ability to grasp context. It can evaluate a sentence, paragraph, or complete page, grasp the underlying themes and concepts, and then generate content that smoothly fits with the existing information. This means that AI copywriting is no longer a mechanical process; it has become a creative one.

Moreover, GPT-4 allows the flexibility to develop content in a range of styles and tones. Whether you require a professional, serious tone for a corporate report or a conversational, pleasant style for a blog article, GPT-4 can deliver. It is not only a tool for generating text; it is a versatile writing partner.

The Impact on Content Creation

AI copywriting has already begun to transform article creation across numerous industries. Marketing, for instance, has experienced a considerable upheaval. Marketers increasingly utilize AI to develop captivating ad copy, engaging email campaigns, and persuasive product descriptions. With GPT-4, the quality of these marketing materials has improved considerably, leading to better conversion rates and more engaging consumer engagements.

Journalism, too, has been influenced by AI. Automated news pieces and reports are becoming increasingly frequent, enabling media firms to cover a greater range of stories fast. While there are real concerns about the influence on traditional media, AI can provide a vital supplement for time-sensitive, data-driven reporting.

In the area of e-commerce, AI-generated product descriptions can save both time and resources, allowing online shops to list and explain a huge assortment of products quickly. This not only streamlines processes but also improves the customer experience, as customers can get specific information about products more simply.

The Human Element

While GPT-4's powers are awe-inspiring, they do raise a fundamental question: what about the human element? Does the rise of AI copywriting harm the livelihood of human writers and content creators?

The answer is subtle. AI is a tremendous tool, but it is not a replacement for human creativity and understanding. It can support and enrich the work of writers, but it cannot reproduce the depth of human thought and passion that permeates the best pieces of literature, journalism, or marketing content. In fact, it is often human writers that train and coach AI systems, ensuring that they produce content that corresponds with a brand's values, tone, and objectives.

Furthermore, the collaboration between AI and humans offers great promise. While AI can generate initial drafts and routine content, people can give the finishing touches, bringing personality and creativity. This collaborative approach allows businesses and content creators to work more efficiently, focusing on the strategic parts of their trade rather than monotonous activities.

The Ethical Dimension

The evolution of AI copywriting also creates ethical problems. As AI gets increasingly skilled at copying human writing, it becomes necessary to evaluate concerns of openness and authenticity. Readers deserve to know if the content they engage with is generated by AI or crafted by humans.

Moreover, the potential exploitation of AI-generated content for propaganda, misinformation, or harmful objectives highlights the need for stringent norms and ethical standards. It is incumbent upon the AI community and society at large to adopt responsible AI practices that safeguard against these hazards.

The Road Ahead

As we explore the realm of GPT-4 and beyond, we find ourselves at an exciting point in the evolution of AI copywriting. The future offers even more sophisticated AI systems that will continue to change content creation, communication, and creativity.

For organizations, marketers, and content providers, embracing this technology is not simply an option; it's a must. The efficiency, variety, and quality that AI copywriting offers are vital to remain competitive in today's digital world.

However, as we go forward, it is necessary to strike a delicate balance between the benefits of AI and the preservation of the human touch. Embracing AI should not decrease the importance of human creativity, intelligence, and craftsmanship. The actual power lies in the collaboration between man and machine, when the distinctive capabilities of each are utilized to produce something truly exceptional.

The progress of AI copy-writing, embodied by GPT-4, is a testament to the immense potential of artificial intelligence. It has already revolutionized content creation across industries, creating new opportunities and difficulties. As we traverse this brave new world, we must do so with responsibility and a deep understanding of the ethical implications, ensuring that the synthesis of human and AI innovation leads to a better, more innovative future.

ENHANCING CREATIVITY WITH AI-GENERATED IDEAS

Creativity is the lifeblood of innovation, powering the engine of progress across industries and human endeavors. From art and design to technology and business, creativity is the driving force that propels us forward. While the wellspring of human imagination is boundless, it's fascinating to consider how AI-generated ideas can enhance and elevate our creative potential.

The Creative Revolution:

The history of human creativity is marked by revolutions, each pushing the boundaries of what was thought possible. The Renaissance, for instance, was a profound artistic and intellectual movement that brought forth breathtaking masterpieces, such as da Vinci's Mona Lisa and Michelangelo's David. Fast forward to the digital age, and we witness a new revolution – one powered by AI.

AI, a technological marvel, has been rapidly evolving, making leaps and bounds in various fields. One of its most transformative applications is the generation of ideas. By analyzing vast amounts of data, AI algorithms can identify patterns, make connections, and generate ideas that may elude human creativity. This opens up a world of possibilities across sectors.

Enhancing Human Creativity:

AI is not here to replace human creativity, but rather to augment it. By leveraging AI-generated ideas, individuals can access a treasure trove of inspiration that can boost their own creative processes. Here's how:

Idea generation and brainstorming: When tasked with generating fresh ideas, AI can serve as an invaluable brainstorming partner. By analyzing trends, market data, and historical insights, AI can offer a plethora of innovative concepts that can spark human creativity.

Cross-pollination of disciplines: AI doesn't have limitations based on industry or field. It can draw inspiration from various domains and connect seemingly unrelated concepts. This cross-disciplinary approach can lead to groundbreaking ideas that humans might never have considered.

Efficient content creation: In the world of content creation, whether it's writing, graphic design, or music composition, AI can aid in generating initial drafts or prototypes, providing a foundation upon which human creativity can build.

Rapid prototyping and experimentation: AI-powered simulations can quickly produce prototypes, enabling creators to test and iterate on ideas more efficiently. This reduces the fear of failure and encourages experimentation.

Data-driven insights: AI can analyze user data, market trends, and consumer behavior to identify opportunities for innovation. It can provide valuable insights that inform the creative process.

AI-Generated Ideas in Action:

Several industries have already harnessed AI-generated ideas to revolutionize their creative processes:

Art and Design: AI-generated art, such as the works of AI artist Robbie Barrat, combines technology and human vision to create striking pieces that push the boundaries of artistic expression.

Healthcare: AI algorithms are assisting medical researchers in identifying potential drug candidates and predicting disease outbreaks, driving innovation in the field of medicine.

Music: AI-generated compositions and remixes have opened up new frontiers in music, enabling artists to experiment with novel sounds and melodies.

Marketing: AI-driven content recommendation engines are helping marketers tailor their messages to specific audiences, enhancing customer engagement and conversion rates.

Film and Entertainment: AI-generated scripts and storylines are being explored to create unique narratives and experiences that captivate audiences.

Embracing the Future:

AI-generated ideas are not a threat to human creativity but rather a powerful tool to amplify it. By combining the limitless imagination of humans with the data-crunching capabilities of AI, we can unlock unprecedented creative potential. The future is exciting, filled with uncharted territories where AI and human creativity coalesce to spark the next great Renaissance.

As we move forward, we must embrace this synergy, fostering a harmonious partnership between humans and AI to push the boundaries of what is creatively possible. The key lies in recognizing AI as a facilitator, a muse, and an accelerator of human creativity. In doing so, we embark on a journey that promises to reshape industries, elevate art, and transform our world into a realm of boundless creative possibilities.

CHAPTER FIVE

SEO COPYWRITING WITH AI

Unlocking the power of search engine optimization (SEO) is essential in today's digital landscape. This chapter delves into the intricate art of optimizing content to rise in search engine rankings, employing practical strategies, real-world examples, and compelling statistics to guide you toward online success.

Unleashing the Potential of SEO

Before we dive into the intricacies, let's underscore the significance of SEO. In a world where 5.6 billion Google searches occur daily, harnessing SEO is non-negotiable. It's the compass leading your target audience to your digital doorstep. But how can you make your content

SEO-friendly without sounding robotic or sacrificing readability?

Keywords: The Bedrock of SEO

Keywords are the foundation of SEO. To find the right keywords for your content, tools like Google Keyword Planner and SEMrush are invaluable. For example, if you're writing a blog about sustainable fashion, keywords like "ethical clothing" or "sustainable fashion brands" can work wonders.

Quality Content Is King

Google prioritizes content quality, not keyword stuffing. In 2021, a study by Backlinko revealed that the average first-page result contains 1,447 words. So, instead of focusing on a specific keyword density, concentrate on delivering in-depth, informative content that your audience craves.

Engaging Titles and Meta Descriptions

Crafting captivating titles and meta descriptions is an art. Ahrefs found that pages with a title tag containing 15-40 characters have higher click-through rates. Ensure your titles are concise, relevant, and compelling, while meta descriptions should offer a sneak peek into the content's value.

Optimizing Multimedia

Don't overlook images and videos. Compress images to enhance page speed, and use alt text with descriptive keywords. Videos are gaining traction; a report by Cisco predicted that by 2022, videos would constitute 82% of internet traffic. Thus, optimizing video content is essential for SEO.

User Experience Matters

Google is adamant about providing a superior user experience. A slow-loading website can be detrimental. Google's Speed Update in 2018 emphasized mobile page speed. According to Google, if a page takes more than 3 seconds to load, 53% of mobile users will abandon it. Therefore, optimizing page speed is not only an SEO tactic but also a user-friendly approach.

Backlinks: Quality Over Quantity

Backlinks remain a cornerstone of SEO. A study by Moz found a high correlation between the number of backlinks and organic search traffic. However, quality surpasses quantity. A single authoritative backlink can outweigh dozens of low-quality ones.

Local SEO

For businesses with physical locations, local SEO is pivotal. According to HubSpot, 46% of all Google searches are seeking local information. Make sure your business is listed on Google My Business and other relevant directories.

Algorithm Updates and Adaptation

Google's algorithms are continually evolving. In 2021, Google released a core update in June that significantly impacted search results. Staying updated and adapting to algorithm changes is vital for maintaining your search rankings.

Analyzing SEO Performance

Measuring the effectiveness of your SEO efforts is crucial. Utilize tools like Google Analytics and Search

Console to track website traffic, keyword rankings, and user behavior. These insights help you fine-tune your SEO strategy.

Case Study: Moz's Whiteboard Friday

A prime example of successful SEO content is Moz's "Whiteboard Friday" series. They consistently deliver in-depth, informative content about SEO, and their dedication to quality has earned them high search rankings and a loyal audience.

Key SEO Statistics

- 75% of users never scroll past the first page of search results (HubSpot).

- 68% of online experiences begin with a search engine (BrightEdge).

- Voice search is on the rise, with 40% of adults using it daily (Location World).

- 80% of consumers believe that brands providing custom content are more trustworthy (True North Custom).

Therefore, optimizing content for search engines is a multifaceted strategy that combines keyword research, high-quality content, user experience, and adaptability. While SEO can be complex, mastering it will propel your digital presence to new heights, attracting a broader audience and driving organic traffic to your website. Stay committed to your SEO efforts, and success in the digital realm will be within your reach.

AI-DRIVEN KEYWORD RESEARCH

Search engine optimization (SEO) stands as a cornerstone for businesses looking to increase their online visibility. The key to successful SEO lies in understanding the language of search engines and aligning your content with the queries of your target audience. Herein, AI-driven keyword research has emerged as a game-changer, revolutionizing the way businesses approach SEO strategy.

The Evolution of Keyword Research

Traditionally, keyword research involved manually sifting through data to identify relevant keywords and phrases that users entered into search engines. This time-consuming and often imprecise process has been drastically transformed by AI. With machine learning algorithms and natural language processing, AI-driven keyword research tools can swiftly analyze vast datasets to identify high-value keywords, uncover search trends, and predict user behavior.

HARNESSING AI FOR KEYWORD RESEARCH

Efficiency and Precision: AI-driven tools, such as Ahrefs and SEMrush, can process and evaluate a multitude of keywords at an unprecedented speed. This efficiency allows businesses to uncover new keyword opportunities, track keyword performance, and adapt their strategies accordingly.

Competitive Analysis: AI tools excel at analyzing competitors' strategies. By studying their keywords, content, and backlinks, businesses can gain insights to outperform their rivals.

User Intent Prediction: AI can understand user intent, not just keywords. It identifies the underlying motivations behind search queries and suggests content that matches the user's needs. For instance, if a user searches for "best smartphones," AI can distinguish between someone looking to buy a smartphone and someone seeking reviews.

Statistics on AI-Driven Keyword Research

According to a study by BrightEdge, 80% of businesses that have implemented AI in their SEO strategy have reported a significant increase in organic search rankings.

HubSpot reports that 61% of marketers say improving SEO and growing their organic presence is their top inbound marketing priority.

SEMrush data reveals that websites that use AI-powered keyword research tools see an average 20% increase in their organic search traffic in the first six months.

EXAMPLES OF AI SUCCESS STORIES

Coca-Cola: Coca-Cola employed an AI-driven tool to optimize their SEO strategy, resulting in a 24% increase in organic search traffic within just one year.

Amazon: By using AI to tailor their product listings and keywords, Amazon has seen substantial growth in their organic search visibility.

AI-driven keyword research has transformed SEO from a labor-intensive task into a streamlined and data-driven process. The efficiency, precision, and insights AI brings to keyword research allow businesses to stay ahead of the curve and adapt to evolving search engine algorithms. By harnessing the power of AI, companies can achieve higher search rankings, increased organic traffic, and a competitive edge in the digital marketplace. As the statistics and examples demonstrate, AI-driven keyword research is not just a luxury but a necessity for any business looking to thrive in the digital age.

CRAFTING SEO-FRIENDLY COPY WITH AI

Crafting SEO-Friendly Copy with AI is a practical and effective approach to improve your website's visibility and drive organic traffic. By following these professional steps, you can harness the power of AI to create compelling content that resonates with both search engines and your target audience.

Keyword Research: Begin by conducting thorough keyword research to identify relevant search terms. Tools like Google Keyword Planner and Ahrefs can help you find high-traffic keywords. For example, if you have a gardening website, you might discover that "organic gardening tips" is a popular keyword.

AI-Powered Content Generation: Utilize AI writing tools such as OpenAI's GPT-3 to generate content ideas. For instance, you can input your target keyword, and the AI can provide a list of potential article titles and content outlines.

Content Optimization: After generating content, optimize it for SEO. This includes placing your target keyword strategically throughout the text. Aim for a keyword density of around 1-2%, ensuring that the text flows naturally. For example, if your keyword is "organic gardening tips," it should be seamlessly integrated into the content.

Semantic SEO: AI can help you discover semantically related keywords to enhance the context of your content.

Tools like LSIGraph can provide related keywords like "composting," "soil enrichment," and "sustainable gardening," which can be incorporated to strengthen your content's relevancy.

Readability and User Experience: Remember that SEO-friendly copy should not sacrifice readability. Use AI tools like Grammarly to check for grammar and spelling errors, ensuring a smooth reading experience.

Header Tags and Meta Descriptions: Optimize header tags (H1, H2, H3) with your target keyword and include it in the meta description. AI tools like Yoast SEO can assist in crafting meta descriptions that encourage clicks.

Internal and External Links: AI can help identify relevant internal and external links to include in your content. For instance, if you're writing about organic gardening, link to previous articles on your site and authoritative sources about sustainable agriculture.

Content Length: AI can analyze the ideal content length for your topic based on top-ranking pages. For example, it may recommend that your gardening tips article should be at least 1,500 words for better SEO performance.

Image Optimization: AI tools like TinyPNG can compress and optimize images for faster page loading, which is a crucial SEO factor. Ensure images are named descriptively, such as "organic-gardening-tools.jpg."

Regular Updates: AI can track the performance of your content and suggest updates or revisions. Tools like Google Analytics and SEMrush can provide valuable insights into which pages are driving the most traffic.

Example of AI's Impact: A study by HubSpot found that content with a word count between 2,250 and 2,500 words tends to rank the highest on search engine results pages (SERPs). AI can assist in recommending the optimal content length for your specific topics, improving your chances of ranking higher in search results.

AI can be a powerful ally in crafting SEO-friendly copy. By using AI tools for research, content generation, and optimization, you can enhance your website's visibility, attract more organic traffic, and ultimately, improve your online presence.

CHAPTER SIX

SOCIAL MEDIA COPYWRITING

Crafting engaging social media posts is essential for capturing your audience's attention and driving meaningful interactions. Here are professional, practical steps to help you create compelling content:

Know Your Audience: Understand your target audience's demographics, interests, and pain points. For example, if you're promoting fitness products, know that 80% of your audience may be between 18-35 years old, interested in health, and seeking workout motivation.

Set Clear Objectives: Define the purpose of your post. Are you aiming to inform, entertain, inspire, or sell? Objectives guide content creation. For instance, if you're a fashion brand, a post showcasing a new collection should aim to inspire and inform.

Create Eye-Catching Visuals: High-quality images or videos are more likely to grab attention. For instance, a crisp, well-lit photo of a mouth-watering dish can draw foodies in faster than a blurry image.

Craft Captivating Headlines: Your post's title or caption must be concise and intriguing. Use action words and ask questions. For a travel blog, "Ready to Explore Paradise?" could pique interest.

Tell a Story: Stories resonate with audiences. Share personal experiences, customer testimonials, or industry success stories. For a tech company, a post about a customer's journey solving a problem using your product can engage your audience emotionally.

Use Hashtags Strategically: Research and employ relevant hashtags to increase discoverability. For example, a post about pet care can benefit from popular tags like #PetLovers or #FurBabies.

Engage with Followers: Respond to comments and messages promptly. Encourage conversations and ask questions to boost engagement. If you run a business consultancy, responding to a comment with "What challenges do you face in your business?" encourages dialogue.

Post at Optimal Times: Analyze your audience's online activity to determine the best posting times. Tools like Buffer or Hootsuite can help you schedule posts accordingly.

A/B Testing: Experiment with different content formats, posting times, and captions. Track engagement metrics to identify what works best. Adjust your strategy accordingly.

Measure and Analyze: Use analytics tools to monitor post performance. Key metrics include likes, shares, comments, and click-through rates. For instance, if a post received 30% more shares than your average, analyze why and replicate the approach.

Crafting engaging social media posts is a dynamic process. Keep refining your strategy based on what resonates with your audience. These steps, supported by data and examples, will help you create content that not only captures attention but also fosters a loyal online community.

GENERATING BUZZWORTHY CONTENT WITH AI

Creating buzzworthy content is essential for engaging your audience and driving brand visibility. Artificial Intelligence (AI) has emerged as a powerful tool for content creators, enabling them to produce high-impact, attention-grabbing content. Here are practical steps, supported by examples and statistics, to help you harness the potential of AI in generating buzzworthy content.

Leverage AI for Data Insights: Start by using AI to analyze vast datasets and uncover trending topics and keywords. Tools like Google Trends and BuzzSumo can provide valuable insights into what's currently capturing the public's attention.

Example: Google Trends revealed that during the COVID-19 pandemic, "home workouts" gained significant traction. A fitness brand could leverage this insight to create content around home workouts.

Personalize Content with AI: Tailor your content to your audience using AI-driven personalization. According to Statista, personalized marketing campaigns can boost engagement rates by up to 17%.

Example: Amazon's product recommendations based on user behavior illustrate how AI personalization can enhance the user experience and drive sales.

Automate Content Creation: AI-powered content generators, like GPT-3, can produce compelling articles, social media posts, and even video scripts. These tools save time and ensure consistency.

Example: AI-generated content can be used to draft routine news articles or product descriptions, allowing human writers to focus on more creative, high-impact pieces.

Harness Visual Content: Use AI tools like Canva or Adobe Sensei to create eye-catching visuals and videos. Visual content gets 94% more views than text-only content.

Example: Instagram filters and image enhancement tools utilize AI to transform ordinary photos into captivating visuals.

Predictive Analytics for Timing: AI can predict the best times to post content for maximum visibility and engagement. HubSpot reports that posting at optimal times can increase social media click-through rates by 25%.

Example: Social media management tools like Hootsuite use AI algorithms to suggest the best posting times for each platform.

A/B Testing with AI: Optimize your content's performance through A/B testing using AI-driven tools like Optimizely. These tools help determine which headlines, images, or CTAs resonate best with your audience.

Example: Booking.com uses A/B testing to fine-tune the design and content of its website, resulting in increased bookings.

Embrace Chatbots for Customer Interaction: AI-powered chatbots can engage with customers 24/7. According to IBM, 80% of customer queries can be answered by a chatbot.

Example: Starbucks' chatbot allows customers to place orders and make inquiries, enhancing the customer experience and driving sales.

By integrating AI into your content strategy, you can stay ahead of the curve and create content that resonates with your target audience. These steps, accompanied by real-world examples and statistics, highlight the practical ways AI can help you produce buzzworthy content that captivates your audience and boosts brand awareness.

MAXIMIZING YOUR SOCIAL MEDIA REACH

Maximizing your social media reach is essential for growing your online presence and engaging with your target audience. To achieve this, you should follow these professional and practical steps, supported by examples and relevant statistics:

Define Your Target Audience:

Start by identifying your ideal audience. Who are they? What are their interests, demographics, and online behaviors? For instance, if you're a fitness influencer, your target audience might be fitness enthusiasts aged 18-35.

Choose the Right Platforms:

Focus your efforts on platforms where your target audience is most active. Statistically, as of 2022, Facebook remains the largest social media platform, with over 2.8 billion monthly active users. However, platforms like Instagram, TikTok, and LinkedIn have been growing significantly and may better suit your niche.

Develop a Content Strategy:

Create high-quality, consistent, and valuable content that resonates with your audience. For example, if you're a food blogger, share mouth-watering recipes, behind-the-scenes cooking videos, and engaging food facts.

Use Visuals:

Posts with visuals, such as images and videos, perform better. On average, tweets with images receive 150% more retweets than text-only tweets.

Optimize Posting Times:

Analyze your audience's online activity to determine the best times to post. Tools like Facebook Insights or Twitter Analytics provide valuable data. For instance, you might find that posting on Instagram at 7 PM on Wednesdays garners higher engagement.

Engage and Respond:

Interact with your followers. Promptly respond to comments and messages. A study revealed that 71% of consumers who have a positive social media experience with a brand are likely to recommend it to others.

Utilize Hashtags:

Employ relevant hashtags to increase the discoverability of your content. On Instagram, posts with at least one hashtag receive 12.6% more engagement.

Collaborate and Cross-Promote:

Partner with influencers or complementary businesses in your industry. Cross-promotion can introduce your content to a new and relevant audience.

Run Paid Campaigns:

Invest in paid advertising. For instance, Facebook ads can reach a highly targeted audience, and Instagram's sponsored posts can significantly increase your visibility.

Analyze and Adjust:

Regularly review your social media analytics. Identify what's working and what isn't. Make data-driven adjustments to your strategy.

Maximizing your social media reach requires careful planning, consistent effort, and a focus on data-driven decision-making. By targeting the right audience, creating engaging content, and utilizing various strategies, you can expand your social media reach and ultimately achieve your online goals. Keep in mind that the social media landscape is constantly evolving, so staying updated with the latest trends and statistics is crucial for long-term success.

Part III: Advanced Copy-writing

Techniques

CHAPTER SEVEN

A/B TESTING AND OPTIMIZATION

Split testing, also known as A/B testing, is a potent tool in the realm of marketing and website optimization. It enables businesses to compare two or more variations of a webpage, email campaign, or ad, in order to determine which one performs better. By following the steps listed below, you can leverage the power of split testing to enhance your marketing efforts and drive impressive results.

Define Clear Objectives:

Begin by establishing clear goals for your split test. Are you looking to boost click-through rates, increase conversions, or enhance user engagement? For instance, if you're running an e-commerce website, your objective might be to increase the click-through rate on product pages.

Create Variations:

Develop distinct variations of the element you want to test. For example, if you're testing a call-to-action (CTA) button, create different versions with varying colors, text, and placement.

Randomly Segment Your Audience:

To ensure unbiased results, divide your audience randomly into groups. This can be done using tools like Google Optimize or Optimizely. Segmenting users this way ensures that both variations are exposed to the same demographics and user behavior.

Implement the Test:

Run the split test for a specific period. For instance, test Variation A and Variation B of a landing page for two weeks to gather sufficient data.

Monitor and Analyze:

Collect data on key metrics such as conversion rates, bounce rates, and engagement levels for both variations. Utilize analytical tools to compare results. For example, if Variation A had a 5% conversion rate while Variation B had 7%, you can confidently conclude that Variation B is the more effective choice.

Statistical Significance:

Ensure that your results are statistically significant. Tools like Google Optimize can help determine when the sample size is large enough to draw valid conclusions.

Implement the Winner:

Once a variation proves statistically superior, implement it permanently. This could mean adopting a particular email subject line that generated a 20% higher open rate, or rolling out a landing page with a 10% higher conversion rate.

Continual Testing:

Don't stop with one test. The true power of split testing lies in its iterative nature. Continue to refine and optimize your content based on the insights gained from previous tests.

Statistics show the value of split testing. According to a study by Econsultancy, 62% of businesses reported that they saw an uplift in conversion rates due to split testing. In another case, the Obama campaign famously leveraged A/B testing to raise an additional $60 million in contributions during his 2012 presidential campaign.

Split testing is a robust strategy that can have a significant impact on your marketing efforts. By following these professional steps and analyzing the data, you can harness the power of split testing to make informed decisions, improve your ROI, and continually enhance your marketing campaigns.

AI-DRIVEN A/B TESTING AND ANALYSIS

AI-driven A/B testing and analysis is a powerful approach for optimizing digital marketing campaigns, websites, and user experiences. It leverages artificial intelligence to enhance the efficiency and effectiveness of A/B tests. Here are detailed steps for implementing

AI-driven A/B testing and analysis, along with practical examples and relevant statistics:

DATA COLLECTION AND PREPARATION:

◆ Collect user data and relevant metrics from your website or app.

◆ Utilize AI to clean and preprocess the data for accurate analysis.

Example: Gather click-through rates (CTR) and conversion rates from two versions of a landing page.

HYPOTHESIS GENERATION:

◆ Formulate hypotheses regarding potential improvements or changes in your design or content.

Example: Hypothesize that changing the color of a call-to-action button will increase CTR.

EXPERIMENT DESIGN:

◆ Create A/B test variants based on your hypotheses, ensuring random assignment of users to each variant.

Example: Design two landing page variants – A (blue button) and B (green button).

AI-POWERED TESTING:

◆ Utilize machine learning algorithms to automate the testing process.

◆ AI can analyze large datasets much faster and more accurately than traditional methods.

Example: AI determines which button color results in a higher CTR by processing vast user interactions.

CONTINUOUS MONITORING:

◆ Use AI to continuously monitor the A/B test in real-time, allowing for quick adjustments.

Example: AI alerts when statistical significance is reached, indicating a clear winner.

STATISTICAL SIGNIFICANCE:

- AI can calculate statistical significance more precisely, reducing the risk of false positives or negatives.

Example: AI determines that Variant B with the green button has a 10% higher CTR with 95% confidence.

SEGMENTATION AND PERSONALIZATION:

- Employ AI to segment users based on behavior and personalize content accordingly.

Example: Users who prefer video content receive video-based CTAs while text-loving users see text-based CTAs.

ITERATIVE TESTING:

- Implement an iterative testing strategy, using AI insights from one test to inform the next.

Example: After successful A/B testing, iterate by experimenting with button size.

PERFORMANCE TRACKING:

◆ Continuously track and measure key metrics such as conversion rates, bounce rates, and revenue.

Example: After implementing the green button, track how it affects the overall revenue and user engagement.

OUTCOME ANALYSIS:

◆ Utilize AI for in-depth analysis of the A/B test results and draw actionable insights.

Example: AI reveals that the green button resulted in a 15% increase in revenue.

IMPLEMENTATION AND SCALING:

◆ Implement the winning variant across the entire platform and scale up successful AI-driven A/B testing.

Example: Deploy the green button across all relevant pages, driving consistent improvements.

CONTINUOUS LEARNING:

♦ Foster a culture of continuous learning, adapting strategies based on AI-driven insights.

Example: Regularly revisit and retest elements of your website to stay competitive.

AI-driven A/B testing and analysis can yield impressive results. In a case study by a leading e-commerce company, implementing AI-driven A/B testing increased conversion rates by 20%, resulting in a $2 million boost in annual revenue. By following these steps and leveraging AI capabilities, businesses can make data-driven decisions and continually optimize their online presence.

CONTINUOUS IMPROVEMENT STRATEGIES

Continuous improvement is a fundamental concept that drives organizational success in today's competitive landscape. It involves making incremental enhancements to processes, products, and services to boost efficiency, quality, and customer satisfaction. To implement an effective continuous improvement strategy, consider the following steps.

Set Clear Objectives: Begin by defining specific, measurable, achievable, relevant, and time-bound (SMART) objectives. For instance, reduce product defects by 10% within six months.

Data Collection and Analysis: Collect relevant data to understand current processes. Employ statistical tools like Pareto charts and control charts to identify areas for improvement. For instance, if customer complaints highlight a specific product flaw, analyze these complaints to pinpoint root causes.

Kaizen Events: Implement Kaizen events – short, focused improvement projects. Gather cross-functional teams to brainstorm and address specific issues, aiming for quick wins. For example, streamline the order fulfillment process to reduce lead times.

Lean Principles: Apply lean principles to eliminate waste. Examples of waste include overproduction, excess inventory, and unnecessary motion. By minimizing waste, you increase efficiency. Toyota is a prime example, having cut waste and improved production.

Six Sigma: Utilize Six Sigma methodologies for process improvement. Measure the sigma level of a process and work to achieve Six Sigma quality, which means fewer than 3.4 defects per million opportunities. General Electric has famously used Six Sigma to save billions.

Total Quality Management (TQM): Embrace TQM, focusing on customer satisfaction and employee involvement. This approach can reduce defects and enhance the overall quality of products and services.

Employee Involvement: Engage employees at all levels to foster a culture of continuous improvement. Empower them to identify and address issues, as they are closest to the processes. Google's "20% time" is a notable example, allowing employees to dedicate a portion of their workday to personal projects that contribute to innovation.

Benchmarking: Compare your organization's performance with industry leaders. Benchmarking helps identify areas where you're falling behind and where improvements are needed.

Technology Integration: Leverage technology for automation and data-driven decision-making. For example, integrate an enterprise resource planning (ERP) system to streamline various processes.

Feedback Loop: Establish a feedback loop with customers to understand their evolving needs. Amazon, for instance, continuously seeks customer feedback and adapts its services accordingly.

Regular Audits: Conduct regular internal audits to ensure compliance with established procedures. Correct deviations promptly to prevent recurring issues.

Key Performance Indicators (KPIs): Monitor and evaluate performance using KPIs. For example, track defect rates, on-time delivery, and customer satisfaction scores.

Implementing continuous improvement strategies leads to impressive results. For instance, the Japanese company Toyota saw a 50% reduction in defects and a 60% increase in productivity after adopting Lean principles. Additionally, Motorola's Six Sigma initiatives saved the company over $16 billion in a span of a few years.

Continuous improvement is a dynamic process that requires commitment, employee involvement, and data-driven decision-making. By following these detailed and practical steps, organizations can achieve operational excellence, enhance customer satisfaction, and stay competitive in an ever-evolving business environment.

CHAPTER EIGHT

PERSUASION AND CONVERSION

At its core, the psychology of persuasion seeks to understand how individuals process information, make choices, and respond to various stimuli. Dr. Robert Cialdini's seminal work, "Influence: The Psychology of Persuasion," elucidates six key principles that drive human decision-making: reciprocity, commitment, social proof, authority, liking, and scarcity. These principles serve as the foundation for effective persuasion strategies.

Applications in Business and Marketing

In the business world, the psychology of persuasion is a vital tool for marketers and sales professionals. It enables them to craft compelling messages and design persuasive campaigns that resonate with the target audience.

Utilizing principles like scarcity, businesses create a sense of urgency, driving customers to make quicker decisions. Additionally, the principle of authority leverages endorsements from credible figures to enhance the perceived value of products or services.

Influence in Personal Relationships

Persuasion psychology is not limited to commerce; it plays a pivotal role in personal relationships as well. The concept of liking underscores the importance of building rapport and trust in interactions. By understanding what makes people like and trust one another, individuals can forge stronger connections and foster meaningful relationships.

Social and Political Impact

The principles of persuasion psychology also find relevance in the political arena. Politicians use these principles to persuade voters, while activists and leaders employ them to mobilize support for social causes. By leveraging the principle of social proof, for example, movements gain momentum as individuals observe others participating in the cause.

Ethical Considerations

While persuasion psychology can be a powerful tool, its use raises ethical questions. The line between persuasion and manipulation can be thin, and it is crucial to exercise this knowledge responsibly. Ensuring that persuasion is guided by ethical principles is imperative to avoid exploiting vulnerabilities in human psychology.

"The Psychology of Persuasion" is a captivating realm of study that offers profound insights into the art of influence. Its principles can be applied in various domains, from business and marketing to personal relationships and social change. Understanding how people think, decide, and react is pivotal for achieving success in an ever-persuasive world. However, it is vital to employ these principles ethically and responsibly, respecting the psychological autonomy of individuals while harnessing the power of persuasion to achieve mutually beneficial outcomes.

PRINCIPLES OF PERSUASION

The psychology of persuasion is a powerful tool in both personal and professional life. Understanding the principles behind persuasion can help individuals influence others, make informed decisions, and navigate the complexities of human interactions. Here, we'll explore this concept with professional insights, practical steps, and illustrative examples.

Reciprocity: People are more likely to say "yes" to those who have previously done them a favor. A classic example is when a restaurant offers free appetizers. This creates a sense of obligation, leading patrons to reciprocate by ordering more food and drinks. Studies show that 46% of customers reciprocate by spending more when given a free sample.

Scarcity: The perception of limited availability can trigger a fear of missing out, making people more likely to make a decision. For instance, stating that a product is available "for a limited time only" can significantly boost sales. In a study, items labeled as "limited stock" sold 29% faster.

Authority: People tend to follow those they perceive as experts. In professional settings, citing industry-specific research or qualifications can enhance your credibility. A study found that participants were 3.5 times more likely to comply with a request from an authoritative figure.

Consistency: Humans prefer to be consistent with their past behavior and commitments. For example, if someone has publicly endorsed a cause, they are more likely to donate to it. A study found that public commitment increases the likelihood of donation by 74%.

Liking: People are more likely to say "yes" to those they like. Building rapport and showing genuine interest in others can significantly influence their decisions. In one study, waitstaff who received positive comments from customers saw a 19% increase in tips.

Social Proof: People often rely on the behavior of others to guide their actions. For example, showcasing customer reviews and testimonials on a website can increase trust and conversions. Research indicates that products with positive reviews are 32% more likely to be purchased

Commitment: Getting a small initial commitment can lead to larger commitments later. In a study, volunteers who agreed to place a small sign in their yards advocating safe driving were more likely to agree to a larger sign promoting the same cause later on.

Emotion: Emotional appeals can be highly persuasive. Craft your message to resonate with your audience's emotions. For instance, a charity campaign focusing on the emotional story of a single child in need can result in higher donations compared to statistics alone.

Reciprocal Concessions: The concept of reciprocity can be leveraged further by offering a concession after an initial request is denied. This approach, known as the "door-in-the-face" technique, can increase compliance.

Timing: The timing of your persuasive efforts matters. Studies show that people are more agreeable when they are in a positive mood. Choose the right moment to make your pitch.

Understanding and applying these principles of persuasion in professional and personal contexts can yield significant results. By harnessing these psychological insights, you can navigate social dynamics, enhance your influence, and make more informed decisions, ultimately leading to greater success in various aspects of your life.

AI POWERED PERSUASION TECHNIQUES

AI-powered persuasion techniques leverage artificial intelligence to influence and persuade individuals effectively. These techniques have gained significant traction in marketing, sales, and customer engagement. Here are some ways to implement AI-powered persuasion techniques:

1. Data Gathering and Analysis:

- *Step*: Collect extensive data about your target audience's preferences and behaviors.

- *Example*: A retail company can gather data on customers' past purchases and online browsing habits.

- *Stat*: 62% of consumers expect personalized offers based on their past interactions (Accenture).

2. Personalized Recommendations:

- *Step:* Utilize AI algorithms to generate tailored product recommendations.

- *Example*: Amazon suggests products based on a user's previous purchases and browsing history.

- *Stat*: Personalized product recommendations can increase conversion rates by 915% (Barilliance).

3. Dynamic Pricing:

- *Step*: Implement AI-driven dynamic pricing to optimize prices in real-time.

- *Example*: Airlines adjust ticket prices based on demand and customer behavior.

- *Stat*: Dynamic pricing can increase revenue by up to 20% (McKinsey).

4. Chatbots and Virtual Assistants:

- *Step*: Deploy AI chatbots to engage and assist customers 24/7.

- *Example*: Many websites use chatbots to answer customer queries instantly.

- *Stat*: Chatbots can reduce customer service costs by up to 30% (IBM).

5. Sentiment Analysis:

- *Step*: Utilize AI to monitor and analyze social media sentiment to gauge public opinion.

- *Example*: Brands track mentions and sentiment on platforms like Twitter to adapt marketing strategies.

- *Stat*: 77% of customers are more likely to buy from brands they follow on social media (Sprout Social).

6. A/B Testing with AI:

- *Step*: Use AI to optimize A/B tests for web content, emails, or ads.

- *Example*: Google Optimize uses AI to find the best-performing web page variations.

- *Stat*: AI-driven A/B testing can increase conversion rates by up to 40% (CXL).

7. Natural Language Generation:

- *Step*: Generate persuasive content using AI-driven natural language generation.

- *Example*: AI can create personalized email copy or product descriptions.

- *Stat*: 61% of marketers believe that AI-powered content generation enhances customer engagement (Forrester).

8. Behavioral Nudges:

- *Step*: Implement behavioral economics principles using AI to nudge decisions.

- *Example*: E-commerce sites use scarcity tactics like "Only 2 left in stock" to encourage quicker purchases.

- *Stat*: Scarcity tactics can boost sales by 226% (Psychology & Marketing).

9. Social Proof:

- *Step*: Utilize AI to showcase social proof, such as user reviews and ratings.

- *Example*: Amazon displays customer reviews to build trust and influence purchasing decisions.

- *Stat*: 90% of consumers consider online reviews as influential as personal recommendations (Zendesk).

10. Continuous Learning:

- *Step*: Train AI models with new data to adapt to changing customer preferences.

- *Example*: Netflix's recommendation system constantly learns from user interactions.

- *Stat*: Netflix's recommendation system saves $1 billion per year by retaining subscribers (The Verge). AI-powered persuasion techniques are transforming how businesses interact with customers. By implementing these steps and leveraging AI, companies can enhance customer engagement, increase conversions, and drive revenue growth.

TURNING CLICKS INTO CONVERSIONS WITH AI

One of the key advantages of using AI for copywriting is its data-driven approach. AI algorithms can analyze vast amounts of data, including user behaviour, preferences, and engagement metrics. This data-driven analysis helps businesses understand their audience better, allowing them to tailor their content to meet the audience's specific needs and desires. This level of personalization can significantly boost the chances of converting clicks into sales or other desired actions.

AI-powered copywriting also excels in predictive analytics. By examining past user interactions and data patterns, AI can anticipate what content or products might interest the user next. This predictive capability enables businesses to present relevant offers and suggestions at the right moment, increasing the likelihood of conversion. For example, an e-commerce site can use AI to recommend products based on a user's previous purchases, enticing them to make additional buys.

Furthermore, AI helps in creating dynamic and engaging content. With Natural Language Processing (NLP) capabilities, AI can generate compelling headlines, product descriptions, and marketing copy. It can even adapt the tone and style of the content to match the preferences of different user segments. This versatility ensures that the content resonates with a broader audience and encourages them to take the desired action.

In addition to enhancing content creation, AI also aids in A/B testing and optimization. By constantly monitoring the performance of different copy variations, AI can identify which messages and formats are most effective. This allows businesses to refine their copywriting strategies over time and optimize their conversion rates.

Moreover, AI chatbots and virtual assistants have become invaluable tools in turning clicks into conversions. These AI-driven applications can engage users in real-time, answering questions, providing product information, and guiding potential customers through the decision-making process. By offering immediate assistance, AI chatbots can help users overcome obstacles and increase the chances of converting.

In conclusion, the integration of AI in copywriting is a game-changer when it comes to turning clicks into conversions. Its data-driven insights, predictive analytics, dynamic content generation, A/B testing, and interactive chatbots are invaluable assets in the digital marketing toolbox. By harnessing the power of AI, businesses can connect with their audience on a deeper level, drive engagement, and ultimately convert more clicks into valuable actions, boosting their bottom line. As the digital landscape continues to evolve, businesses that embrace AI for copywriting will undoubtedly enjoy a competitive advantage in the race for conversions.

CHAPTER NINE

ETHICAL COPYWRITING AND COMPLIANCE

Writing ethical and honest copy is a fundamental principle of effective communication and marketing. It involves creating content that not only engages the audience but also builds trust and credibility. In a world saturated with advertisements and marketing messages, consumers value honesty and authenticity.

First and foremost, ethical copywriting entails telling the truth. Exaggerating or making false claims about a product or service can lead to mistrust and damage your brand's reputation. Instead, focus on highlighting the genuine benefits and features of what you're promoting. When customers feel that you're being truthful, they're more likely to make informed decisions and develop a positive perception of your brand.

Transparency is another essential element of ethical copywriting. Clearly communicate any limitations or potential drawbacks of your product or service. Customers appreciate knowing both the pros and cons, and it shows that you respect their intelligence and value their decision-making process.

Respecting the privacy and consent of your audience is equally crucial. Avoid using personal information without explicit permission. In the age of data privacy concerns, this is not only ethical but also legally necessary. Always provide a clear opt-out option for email newsletters and other forms of communication to give your audience control over their preferences.

Avoid manipulation and fear-based tactics. While creating a sense of urgency can be effective, overusing it or preying on people's insecurities is unethical. Instead, focus on providing valuable information and genuinely helping your customers solve their problems or fulfill their needs.

Furthermore, ethical copywriting respects cultural and social sensitivities. Be aware of the potential impact of your words on diverse audiences, and avoid content that could be considered offensive, discriminatory, or harmful. Your copy should promote inclusivity and diversity.

Finally, ethical and honest copy should align with the values and mission of your brand. Don't compromise your principles for short-term gains. When your copy reflects your brand's integrity and authenticity, you attract like-minded customers who share your values. By being truthful, transparent, and respectful, you can create copy that not only engages but also converts and retains customers. Your reputation and brand's success depend on the integrity of your copywriting, so always strive for the highest ethical standards in your content.

NAVIGATING LEGAL AND REGULATORY CONSIDERATIONS

Legal considerations encompass a wide array of laws and statutes that govern various aspects of our lives. These may include criminal, civil, and administrative laws. Navigating this legal landscape is essential to avoid legal disputes, sanctions, and even criminal charges. For individuals, it means understanding their rights and obligations, from personal contracts to criminal liability. For businesses, it involves adhering to labor laws, intellectual property rights, and tax regulations.

Ignorance of the law is not an excuse, and failing to comply can result in costly lawsuits and reputational damage.

Regulatory considerations, on the other hand, focus on specific industries or sectors. Government agencies set these regulations to protect public safety, the environment, and consumers. Industries such as healthcare, finance, and transportation are heavily regulated to ensure compliance with safety, quality, and ethical standards. Violations can lead to financial penalties, loss of licenses, and even shutdowns. Therefore, organizations must invest in understanding and implementing these regulations to maintain their operations and reputation.

Navigating legal and regulatory considerations requires a proactive approach. This includes seeking legal counsel or compliance experts who can provide guidance and help create internal policies that align with the law. Education and training are essential, as every member of an organization, from executives to front-line employees, plays a role in upholding legal and regulatory compliance. Moreover, it's crucial to stay up-to-date with evolving laws and regulations, as they often change to adapt to new technologies and societal needs. Failure to do so may result in inadvertent violations. Collaborating with industry peers and regulatory bodies can provide valuable insights and facilitate compliance.

The consequences of neglecting legal and regulatory considerations can be severe. Individuals can face fines, imprisonment, or the forfeiture of their assets. For businesses, non-compliance can lead to class-action lawsuits, regulatory fines, and a tarnished reputation, which can be difficult to recover from.

MAINTAINING TRUST WITH YOUR AUDIENCE

Trust is a precious commodity. Whether you're a business, a public figure, or simply an individual with a social media presence, establishing and preserving trust with your audience is paramount. Trust is the cornerstone of effective communication, successful relationships, and a positive reputation. Here's how you can maintain trust with your audience:

1. Transparency: Open and honest communication is the bedrock of trust. Be forthright about your intentions, actions, and any conflicts of interest. When your audience believes that you have nothing to hide, they're more likely to trust you.

2. Consistency: Consistency in your words and actions breeds trust. When you consistently deliver on your promises and uphold your values, your audience will rely on you. Inconsistent behavior erodes trust quickly.

3. Quality and Integrity: Provide high-quality content, products, or services, and do so with integrity. This combination not only builds trust but also enhances your reputation. Quality work demonstrates your commitment to excellence, while integrity shows you're guided by strong moral principles.

4. Empathy and Respect: Show genuine concern for your audience's needs and feelings. Empathizing with their concerns and treating them with respect goes a long way in building trust. It fosters a sense of connection and reciprocity.

5. Accountability: When you make a mistake, own up to it. Taking responsibility and rectifying errors demonstrates integrity and helps rebuild trust. People are more forgiving of those who admit their faults.

6. Reliability: Consistently meeting deadlines and delivering as promised bolsters trust. If your audience knows they can depend on you, they are more likely to stick with you.

7. Active Listening: Pay attention to your audience's feedback, concerns, and preferences. Demonstrating that you value their input by making changes or improvements based on their feedback shows that you respect and trust them.

8. Avoid Deception: Never resort to deceptive practices or false advertising. Once your audience discovers dishonesty, trust is shattered, and it's challenging to regain.

9. Protect Privacy: Safeguard the personal information of your audience. A breach of privacy can lead to a significant loss of trust. Make it clear how you handle data and adhere to privacy regulations.

10. Maintain Relevance: Stay current and relevant in your field. Providing up-to-date information and adapting to changing circumstances maintains trust in your expertise.

11. Build a Community: Foster a sense of community among your audience. When individuals feel they belong, trust flourishes. Encourage dialogue, shared experiences, and mutual support.

12. Engage Ethically: In the digital age, engagement is crucial. However, be mindful of ethical practices, and avoid spammy or intrusive tactics that can damage your credibility.

Maintaining trust with your audience is an ongoing process that requires commitment and consistency. Building trust takes time and effort, but it's an investment that pays off in loyal followers, satisfied customers, and a sterling reputation. Trust is fragile, so handle it with care and integrity to ensure lasting relationships and success in whatever you do.

Part IV: Case Studies and Real-World Examples

CHAPTER TEN

SUCCESS STORIES IN AI-ENHANCED COPYWRITING

From healthcare and finance to manufacturing and retail, businesses are harnessing the capabilities of AI to streamline processes, enhance products and services, and stay ahead of the curve.

One of the primary ways in which industry leaders leverage AI is through automation. AI-powered robots and algorithms are being employed in manufacturing to perform repetitive and dangerous tasks with precision and efficiency. This not only reduces labor costs but also minimizes the risk of accidents. In the financial sector, AI-driven algorithms are used for high-frequency trading, risk assessment, and fraud detection, making transactions more secure and efficient.

Customer service is another area where AI is making a significant impact. Industry giants are employing AI-powered chatbots and virtual assistants to provide 24/7 customer support, answer inquiries, and resolve issues in real-time. This not only enhances the customer experience but also frees up human employees to focus on more complex and value-added tasks.

In the healthcare industry, AI is transforming diagnostics and treatment. Leading companies are using machine learning to analyze vast amounts of medical data and images, aiding in early disease detection and personalized treatment plans. AI is also being used to develop pharmaceuticals more efficiently, potentially accelerating the drug discovery process.

Data-driven decision-making is a fundamental aspect of AI adoption among industry leaders. With AI, businesses can process and analyze massive datasets to gain insights into market trends, customer behavior, and operational efficiency. This data-driven approach helps companies make informed decisions and adapt swiftly to changing market dynamics.

Furthermore, AI plays a crucial role in predictive maintenance for industries like transportation and energy. By monitoring equipment and infrastructure in real-time, AI can predict when maintenance is required, reducing downtime and preventing costly breakdowns.

As industry leaders embrace AI, they are also addressing concerns related to ethics and data privacy. Safeguarding sensitive data and ensuring responsible AI deployment are essential in maintaining public trust and regulatory compliance.

Industry leaders across various sectors are harnessing the power of AI to optimize operations, enhance customer experiences, and gain a competitive edge in an increasingly digital world. By incorporating AI technologies into their strategies, these companies are not only improving efficiency but also driving innovation, leading the way in the ever-evolving landscape of business and technology. As AI continues to advance, its role in shaping the future of industries cannot be underestimated, and businesses that embrace it today are well-positioned for tomorrow's challenges and opportunities.

FROM CLICKS TO PROFITS: CASE STUDY ANALYSES

Companies worldwide are leveraging the power of online platforms to boost their profitability. This phenomenon has given rise to a plethora of case studies, shedding light on the strategies and tactics that have driven these transformations.

One such case study that stands out is Amazon's journey from an online bookstore to an e-commerce giant. Amazon's relentless focus on customer experience and its dedication to data-driven decision-making are two key factors behind its success. By analyzing user data and monitoring buying patterns, Amazon tailors product recommendations, effectively converting clicks into sales. This personalized approach has helped the company achieve tremendous profitability.

Another noteworthy case study is Netflix, which disrupted the entertainment industry. By offering a vast library of content and utilizing algorithms to suggest personalized shows and movies to viewers, Netflix has turned clicks into subscriptions and profits. Their investment in original content, driven by data analytics, has further solidified their position in the market.

The success of Google, the world's most popular search engine, is another fascinating case. Google's pay-per-click advertising model, AdWords, has become a primary revenue source. By matching user searches with relevant ads, Google turns clicks into advertising revenue, a strategy that has fueled its phenomenal growth.

Social media platforms like Facebook have also mastered the art of converting clicks into profits. By collecting user data and providing businesses with targeted advertising opportunities, they monetize user engagement.

Facebook's ability to deliver tailored ads to specific demographics and interests is a prime example of how clicks drive profits in the digital realm.

E-commerce giant Alibaba has not only capitalized on the online marketplace but also extended its reach to cloud computing. Through its subsidiary Alibaba Cloud, the company has leveraged its vast user data and AI capabilities to provide cloud services to businesses, expanding its revenue streams.

These case studies illustrate that converting clicks into profits requires a deep understanding of user behavior and preferences. Data analytics and artificial intelligence play a crucial role in achieving this transformation. Additionally, maintaining a focus on improving the user experience and offering personalized recommendations or advertising creates a virtuous cycle of engagement and profitability.

The shift from clicks to profits is a fundamental aspect of contemporary business success. Case studies of companies like Amazon, Netflix, Google, Facebook, and Alibaba reveal that data-driven strategies, personalized user experiences, and targeted advertising are key drivers of profitability in the digital age. These examples provide valuable insights for businesses aiming to thrive in the ever-evolving online landscape.

KEY TAKEAWAYS FROM SUCCESSFUL CAMPAIGNS

Successful campaigns are the result of careful planning, creative thinking, and effective execution. Whether it's a marketing campaign, political campaign, or a social awareness campaign, there are key takeaways that can be applied to ensure success.

Clear Objectives: The first and foremost key to a successful campaign is to have clear and measurable objectives. What are you trying to achieve? Whether it's increasing brand awareness, driving sales, or raising awareness about an issue, your objectives should be well-defined.

Know Your Audience: Understanding your target audience is essential. Successful campaigns resonate with the people they are trying to reach. Conduct thorough research to identify your audience's needs, preferences, and pain points.

Compelling Storytelling: Storytelling is a powerful tool. Successful campaigns tell a story that engages, captivates, and connects with the audience emotionally. It's not just about facts and figures but about weaving a narrative that sticks.

Consistency: Consistency is key in maintaining a campaign's message and image. All campaign materials, from social media posts to advertisements, should align with the core message and branding.

Multi-Channel Approach: Successful campaigns often utilize multiple channels to reach their target audience. Whether it's through social media, email marketing, print advertising, or events, a multi-channel approach ensures broader reach.

Creativity: Creative thinking can set your campaign apart. Eye-catching visuals, innovative strategies, and unique approaches grab people's attention and make your campaign memorable.

Monitoring and Adaptation: Regular monitoring of campaign performance is crucial. Analytics tools can provide insights into what's working and what isn't. Be ready to adapt and adjust your strategy based on the data.

Engagement and Interaction: Engaging with your audience is vital. Respond to comments, conduct surveys, and encourage user-generated content. Interaction creates a sense of involvement and community.

Timing and Relevance: Timing is everything. Launch your campaign when it's most relevant and likely to gain attention. A campaign about winter coats won't have the same impact in the middle of summer.

Evaluation and Learning: After the campaign is over, it's important to evaluate its success. What worked? What didn't? Use this information to learn and improve for future campaigns.

Testimonials and Social Proof: People trust recommendations from others. Incorporating testimonials, reviews, and endorsements from satisfied customers or supporters can add credibility to your campaign.

Budgeting and Resource Allocation: Allocate your resources wisely. A well-thought-out budget helps ensure that you can execute your campaign effectively and efficiently.

Authenticity: Authenticity is valued by consumers and audiences. Be genuine and transparent in your messaging. Authentic campaigns build trust and credibility.

Flexibility and Adaptability: Be prepared to adapt to unexpected changes or opportunities. Sometimes, a well-timed pivot can make a campaign even more successful.

Post-Campaign Follow-Up: A successful campaign doesn't end with its conclusion. Follow up with your audience to maintain their interest and support.

In conclusion, the success of a campaign hinges on meticulous planning, a deep understanding of the target audience, and a commitment to innovation and engagement. By applying these key takeaways, you can increase the likelihood of achieving your campaign's goals and leaving a lasting impact. Remember, success is not just about the end result but also the journey and the lessons learned along the way.

Part V: The Future of AI in Copywriting

CHAPTER ELEVEN

THE AI REVOLUTION IN COPY-WRITING

As we look to the future, several emerging trends and technologies are poised to shape our world in new and exciting ways.

Artificial Intelligence (AI) and Machine Learning: AI and machine learning continue to revolutionize how we process and interpret data. They're making their mark in industries such as healthcare, finance, and transportation, where they enhance decision-making processes, optimize operations, and even contribute to advancements in personalized medicine and autonomous vehicles.

5G Technology: The rollout of 5G networks is set to transform our connectivity and communication landscape. It promises lightning-fast internet speeds, enabling the

Internet of Things (IoT) to flourish and powering innovations like augmented and virtual reality.

Quantum Computing: Quantum computing is on the horizon, offering the potential to solve complex problems at speeds previously unimaginable. This technology holds the key to breakthroughs in cryptography, drug discovery, and climate modeling.

Blockchain and Cryptocurrency: Beyond cryptocurrencies like Bitcoin, blockchain technology is proving its worth in various sectors. It secures supply chains, ensures transparency in elections, and even transforms how artists are compensated for their work.

Biotechnology and Gene Editing: Biotechnology is making strides in healthcare, enabling precision medicine and gene editing to combat genetic diseases. CRISPR technology, for example, is a powerful tool for editing genes and holds vast potential for treating various ailments.

Renewable Energy and Sustainability: The world is increasingly turning to renewable energy sources like solar and wind power. Sustainability is a driving force in architecture, agriculture, and transportation, with innovations such as electric vehicles and green building practices gaining ground.

Robotics and Automation: Robotics and automation are enhancing efficiency and productivity in manufacturing, healthcare, and logistics. Robots are assisting surgeons in delicate procedures, and self-driving cars are being tested on our roads.

Biometrics and Personalized Security: Biometric technologies, from fingerprint recognition to facial recognition, are becoming ubiquitous in securing our devices, data, and physical spaces. This trend raises questions about privacy and data protection.

Space Exploration: Space exploration is gaining momentum, with private companies entering the race alongside government agencies. Lunar missions, Mars colonization, and asteroid mining are now conceivable goals.

Augmented Reality (AR) and Virtual Reality (VR): AR and VR technologies are creating immersive experiences in gaming, education, and training. They're also revolutionizing architecture and design, allowing professionals to visualize projects in new dimensions.

Cybersecurity: As technology advances, so do cyber threats. Cybersecurity remains a pressing concern, with the development of AI-driven security systems and blockchain-based solutions to protect digital assets.

These emerging trends and technologies are not isolated; they often intersect, creating opportunities for innovative cross-disciplinary solutions. However, they also pose challenges, from ethical considerations to potential job displacement. The rate of change is rapid, and as these trends continue to unfold, it's vital for individuals, businesses, and governments to adapt and navigate this ever-evolving landscape. Embracing these trends thoughtfully, while addressing their associated challenges, is key to shaping a brighter and more technologically advanced future.

PREPARING FOR THE FUTURE OF AI-GENERATED CONTENT

AI-generated content, from articles and artwork to music and advertisements, is becoming increasingly prevalent, prompting us to think about how we should prepare for this new era.

One key aspect of preparing for the future of AI-generated content is understanding its capabilities and limitations. AI can generate vast amounts of text and media quickly, making it a valuable tool for content creation and curation. However, it lacks the nuanced understanding, creativity, and critical thinking that humans possess. This means that while AI can automate many aspects of content production, human creativity and oversight remain essential for crafting meaningful and resonant content.

To harness the power of AI-generated content effectively, individuals and businesses need to adapt their workflows. It's essential to invest in AI tools and platforms that align with your content goals. These tools can streamline the content creation process, help with data analysis, and even automate tasks like content distribution and social media posting.

Moreover, it's vital to cultivate a workforce with AI literacy. Employees should understand how AI works, its applications, and its potential impacts. AI-generated content tools can be used to assist and enhance the work of human creators, not replace them. Therefore, individuals and organizations must promote a culture of collaboration between AI and human creativity.

Ethical considerations are also paramount in the era of AI-generated content. We need to establish clear guidelines and standards for AI use in content creation. This includes transparency in disclosing AI involvement and addressing issues related to intellectual property and plagiarism. AI-generated content should align with ethical principles, ensuring it benefits society and doesn't harm individuals or communities.

As AI-generated content proliferates, we must remain vigilant in combating misinformation and deepfakes. Reliable fact-checking and source verification are crucial to ensure that AI-generated content is accurate and trustworthy. Organizations and platforms should implement mechanisms to verify and label AI-generated content as such, allowing consumers to make informed choices.

The future of AI-generated content promises exciting opportunities for creativity and efficiency, but it also raises challenges and ethical dilemmas. To prepare for this future, we must educate ourselves, adapt our workflows, and prioritize ethics and transparency. By harnessing AI as a creative ally and using it responsibly, we can navigate the evolving landscape of content creation and consumption and continue to deliver meaningful and impactful content to audiences around the world.

STAYING AHEAD IN THE WORLD OF COPYWRITING

Copywriters play a pivotal role in crafting persuasive content that captures the audience's attention and drives desired actions. To excel in this ever-evolving domain, professionals must adapt, innovate, and continuously enhance their skills.

Constant Learning: One of the golden rules of copywriting is never to stop learning. The industry evolves with trends, technologies, and consumer behavior. Staying ahead requires keeping up with the latest developments. Read books, blogs, and attend webinars to stay updated on the latest strategies and tools.

Adapt to Different Mediums: Copywriting isn't confined to one medium. It spans across various platforms, including websites, social media, email, and print. Being proficient in all these mediums is essential. Adapting your writing style to each platform's unique requirements can help you stand out.

Master SEO: Search Engine Optimization (SEO) is a critical aspect of modern copywriting. Understanding how to incorporate keywords effectively and write content that ranks well in search engines is crucial. Stay updated on Google's algorithm changes to ensure your content remains relevant.

Understand Data and Analytics: Copywriters need to be data-driven. Learning how to interpret website analytics, click-through rates, and conversion data can help you make informed decisions about your content strategy. This insight enables you to refine your copy for better results.

Embrace Creativity: Copywriting is both science and art. While data is essential, creativity sets you apart. Developing a unique voice and style will make your copy memorable. Don't be afraid to experiment with different tones, styles, and storytelling techniques.

Build a Personal Brand: In the gig economy, your personal brand matters. Establishing a strong online presence and showcasing your expertise can attract clients and opportunities. Share your knowledge through social media, a personal blog, or guest posting on relevant platforms.

Networking: Copywriting is often a solo endeavor, but networking is invaluable. Connect with fellow copywriters, marketers, and business professionals. Attend industry conferences and join online communities to exchange ideas and potentially land lucrative projects.

Client Relationships: Building strong relationships with clients is a vital skill. Understand their needs and expectations, and communicate effectively to ensure your copy aligns with their vision. A satisfied client is more likely to hire you again or refer you to others.

Continuous Improvement: Feedback is a gift. Embrace criticism and use it as an opportunity to grow. Take online courses or workshops to hone your skills and explore new techniques.

Stay Ethical: In a world where fake news and unethical practices abound, integrity is essential. Be transparent and honest in your copy. Ethical copywriting builds trust with the audience and clients.

In the world of copywriting, staying ahead means being a well-rounded professional who combines creativity, adaptability, and a strong foundation in the basics. Continuous learning, innovation, and personal growth are key to success. The ability to write persuasive, engaging content will always be in demand, but it's the copywriters who keep evolving and refining their skills who truly excel in this field.

CHAPTER TWELVE

CONCLUSION

Artificial Intelligence (AI) is revolutionizing various industries, and copywriting is no exception. In recent years, AI has emerged as a powerful tool for copywriters, helping them craft compelling and effective content. From generating product descriptions to optimizing marketing campaigns, AI offers a wide array of benefits for copywriters. This expository writeup explores the full potential of AI in copywriting.

One of the key advantages of AI in copywriting is its ability to automate repetitive tasks. AI-powered tools can generate content at a scale and speed that humans simply cannot match. For instance, AI can produce product descriptions for an entire catalog in a fraction of the time it would take a human writer. This efficiency not only saves time but also reduces costs for businesses.

AI can also enhance the quality of copywriting. Natural Language Processing (NLP) algorithms allow AI to understand the context and intent of the content it is creating. This enables AI to produce highly relevant and engaging copy that resonates with the target audience. AI can even help in A/B testing to determine which variations of copy perform best, thus refining the messaging for better results.

Another remarkable feature of AI is its ability to tailor content to individual preferences. Personalization is a crucial aspect of effective copywriting, and AI can analyze user data to create customized content. By leveraging data on user behavior and preferences, AI can deliver personalized emails, product recommendations, and marketing messages, significantly improving customer engagement.

AI's contribution to SEO cannot be underestimated. Search engine algorithms are constantly evolving, and AI can assist in optimizing content for better search engine rankings. AI-driven tools can analyze keyword trends, identify the most relevant keywords, and suggest improvements to boost a website's visibility.

Moreover, AI can offer valuable insights into content performance. By tracking metrics such as click-through rates, conversion rates, and engagement levels, AI can provide data-driven feedback to help copywriters refine their strategies. This data-driven approach allows for continuous improvement and more effective content creation.

However, it's important to note that while AI is a powerful tool in copywriting, it is not a replacement for human creativity. Effective copywriting still requires the human touch to infuse creativity, emotion, and brand personality into the content. AI can assist in the drafting and optimization phases, but the initial spark of creativity and the ability to build a brand narrative remain firmly in the domain of human writers.

In conclusion, AI has the potential to revolutionize copywriting by automating repetitive tasks, enhancing content quality, personalizing messages, improving SEO, and providing valuable insights into performance. While it's not a replacement for human creativity, it is a powerful ally for copywriters looking to streamline their processes and deliver more effective content. As technology continues to advance, harnessing the full potential of AI in copywriting will become an essential skill for modern copywriters.

....

Special note to the reader:

Andrew Mark
Wishes you success on your AI Copywriting Journey!